# AUSTRALIA

COOMBE BOOKS

**Design** Teddy Hartshorn
**Commissioning Editor** Andrew Preston
**Editorial** Jane Adams and Gill Waugh
**Production** Ruth Arthur, David Proffit and Sally Connolly
**Director of Production** Gerald Hughes
**Director of Publishing** David Gibbon

CLB 2553
© 1990 Colour Library Books Ltd, Godalming, Surrey, England
All rights reserved
Colour separations by Hong Kong Graphic Arts, Hong Kong
Printed and bound by Leefung Asco Printers Ltd, Hong Kong
ISBN 0 86283 823 1

# AUSTRALIA

COOMBE BOOKS

The continent of Australia: vast, isolated, arid, ancient. In the southwest, forming part of the Western Australian Shield, are rocks that date from the early Precambrian (Archaean) era, 3,000,000,000 years ago when the earth was young, and that had cooled to form a solid crust just 1,600,000,000 years before....

The earth was wreathed in clouds of water vapour, but no rain fell until temperatures could fall below 100°C – boiling point. When the rains finally came to the parched land, they formed the first streams, lakes and, finally, the seas and oceans.

The appearance of life, in the shape of oxygen-producing blue- green algae, was signalled by deposits of ferrous oxide. Once most of the ferrous iron had been oxidised, oxygen was liberated into the atmosphere and, over the millennia, life forms proliferated and diversified. The earth's surface looked different to the one we know today. As the once united continents of the world began to drift apart, Australia formed part of Gondwanaland, a supercontinent that also consisted of South America, Africa, Antarctica and peninsular India. In due course, Australia would stand alone, a landmass of over 7,600,000 square kilometres, washed by the waters of three oceans and four seas.

Uninhabited by man, Australia lay untouched and timeless. The flora and fauna developed in unique ways, and marsupials flourished, isolated from competition with superior placental mammals. Then, about 40,000 or more years ago, man island-hopped his way to the continent, in canoes or rafts, from Southeast Asia. These were the ancestors of the Aborigines and they could possibly have come from more than one racial stock.

It is possible that Chinese astronomers made observations while in Australia in the sixth century B.C.; they are reputed, with greater certainty, to have made a landing near Darwin in 1432. However, both ancient Chinese and Arab documents refer obscurely to a southern land. From the second century B.C., geographers in Europe were speculating on whether there was a gigantic land mass in the southern hemisphere to balance that in the north. In the second century A.D., Ptolemy wrote his *Guide to Geography*, which suggested that the Indian Ocean was bounded by a southern continent. Maps published in Europe during the Middle Ages, and based on Ptolemy's work, would have the legend *Terra incognita*, 'unknown land', marked on their lower borders.

It was Dutch sailors, at the end of the sixteenth century, who found that, if they sailed 5,000 kilometres eastwards from the Cape, before turning north to the Spice Islands (the Moluccas), they would encounter favourable winds to assist their passage. Soon, however, they even started to make landfalls on a strange coast before turning north. Between 25th and 27th October, 1616, men from Dirck Hartog's *Eendracht* landed at Shark Bay and left a memorial there. In 1618, a Dutch skipper wrote that 'this land is a fit point to be made by ships … in order to get a fixed course for Java'. As navigators drew their charts, Western Australia was at last on the map.

But was this land *terra australis incognita*, the 'unknown southern land'? In 1642, the governor general of the Dutch East India Company sent Abel Tasman on a voyage of exploration. Sailing south, then east from Mauritius, he managed to land in Tasmania. Sailing round the south of the island he sailed east to discover New Zealand's South Island. However, it was in vain that he wrote, 'we trust that this is the mainland coast of the unknown south land'. Continuing his journey, he discovered Tonga and Fiji on his way to make port in Indonesia. However, in a second voyage, two years later, he was more successful and travelled along the north coast of Australia from Cape York to North West Cape, although he did think that the former was a part of New Guinea.

In 1769, Captain James Cook carried out his orders to search in the area between 40° and 35° S 'until you discover [*Terra Australis*] or fall in with the eastern side of the land discovered by Tasman and now called New Zealand'. On 19th April, 1770, Cook landed on the east coast of Australia and then sailed round to the north. Now only the south of the continent was still unknown. In 1798-1799, Tasmania was circumnavigated by George Bass and Matthew Flinders. The latter, in 1801-1803, charted the Great Australian Bight and then circumnavigated the island continent itself. It was Flinders who suggested that the land should be called Australia.

In 1786, the British government decided that New South Wales should be settled, and colonization began in 1788. Although the traditional view is that the prime motive for this course of action was to reduce the number of inmates in Great Britain's prisons, the country having recently lost its American colonies, this view is perhaps simplistic. Great Britain at this time was a world power, much concerned with both commercial and strategic considerations. By claiming the land and starting settlement it had pre-empted rival powers. Also, a base was required from which naval forces could protect British interests in the Far East. Convict labour would provide the necessary muscle to tame the hostile environment.

The First Fleet reached Botany Bay on 19th-20th January, 1788. However, the region was found to be totally unsuitable for settlement. Therefore, on 21st January the commander of the expedition, Captain Arthur Phillip, set sail again and reached a bay that Cook had called Port Jackson. Phillip described it as 'the finest harbour in the world, in which a thousand sail of the line may ride in the most perfect security'. On the shores of a small inlet the settlement was established and Phillip called the region Sydney Cove. Around it was to grow the city of Sydney, built in fine style for, as Marine Captain Watkin Tench had written in those far-off days, 'to proceed on a narrow, confined scale in a country of the extensive limits we possess, would be unpardonable ... extent of Empire demands grandeur of design'.

In the mid-1820s, Britain had taken possession of the entire continent, fearing expansionist French and even American aims. By 1830, approximately 50,000 male and 8,000 female convicts had landed in Australia. But public opinion in the mother country was beginning to turn against a system that assigned convicts to colonists and looked rather too close to slavery. Transportation to eastern Australia ended in 1852 and to Western Australia in 1868. In total, 151,000 convicts were sent to the east and 10,000 to the west of the country.

It was obvious to men like John Macarthur that wool was going to be one of the nation's primary resources, but the gradual extension of pastureland had an adverse effect upon the Aborigines and their way of life. Bloodshed was often the result of this conflict of interests. In Tasmania, the Aborigines eventually suffered extinction, as they had nowhere to retreat before the white man's rapacious expansion. On the mainland, however, they were able to fade away into the remote areas of bush and outback.

The potential for development in Australia was immense. There were vast tracts of land; there were the men available for work; there were people in other countries willing to buy Australian products, but money was required for the investment necessary to stimulate the economy. Then, in 1851, in southern New South Wales, came a discovery which transformed the country in men's eyes from a land of servitude and hardship to the archetypal land of opportunity – gold!

For over a decade, from the 1850s, the gold mines of Victoria and New South Wales produced over 40 per cent of world output. The wealth that accrued helped in many schemes, including the building of railways and cities and the supply of water and gas to the latter. The country's mineral wealth was to prove bounteous indeed. Today, Australia also produces silver, diamonds, uranium, tungsten, tin, nickel, coal, bauxite, copper, iron ore, lead, manganese, mineral sands (monazite, rutile, ilmenite and zircon), phosphate and zinc.

Traditionally, the wealth of the nation has relied heavily on sheep. In 1797, John Macarthur imported a few Spanish merinos. Within twenty years of this humble beginning, the sheep population had grown to 120,000. Today, this has risen to a staggering 135 million head, which represents fourteen per cent of the world's total.

Perhaps one of the strange facets of Australia's human population is that, for all the continent's huge size, most of the people live near the coast and within a few main centres. In fact, more than 50 per cent live in the spreading urban masses of Melbourne and Sydney alone, and 70 per cent live within eleven major cities with populations of over 100,000 people. These are the Federal capital, Canberra; six of the State capitals – Sydney, Melbourne, Adelaide, Perth, Hobart and Brisbane – and the others are the Gold Coast in Queensland, Wollongong and Newcastle in New South Wales and Geelong in Victoria. The only State capital with a population of under 100,000 is Darwin, in the Northern Territory. There is still, however, a thriving rural community in Australia because so much of the country's prosperity relies on farming and mining carried out in inland areas.

When the men from the First Fleet landed in January 1788, it was intended that they should be self-sufficient in food. On their first day in Botany Bay they found poor soil, a poor harbour and a lack of drinking water. Hardship stared them straight in the face for the first time. The settlers who followed often fared little better in a land which seemed both inhospitable and pitiless.

When there wasn't a drought there was flood, and when there wasn't flood there was fire. The threat of both remains: in the 'Ash Wednesday' fires of 1983, seventy-six people were killed in South Australia and Victoria, and 750,000 hectares of pastureland and forest were destroyed, along with 2,000 houses and several small towns. The final cost of the damage was estimated at $390,000,000.

Outside the cities and the settled urban life lies the Australian bush. Here, the unique flora and fauna of the country can continue to exist with the minimum of interference from man and his imported livestock. The animal life is particularly distinctive. During the glacial periods of the Pleistocene era, 600,000 years ago, the mighty oceans of this planet froze at the north and south poles, which resulted in a fall in the water level elsewhere in the world. Out of the receding waters rose a land bridge, uniting Australia with New Guinea and Tasmania. Hence there is a similarity in the forms of animal life between these regions. But, throughout the Cenozoic era – some 70,000,000 years – Australia has remained separate from the Indonesian Archipelago. Therefore, the fauna of the island continent is unrivalled as a home to the marsupials, such as the koala and kangaroo, and to the only two living monotremes in the world: the echidna and the platypus.

Australia's present fauna is a source of endless delight to tourist and naturalist alike. Records show that there are perhaps 108 species of placental mammals; 125 marsupials; 950 birds, including parrots, cockatoos, the emu and the lyrebird; two monotremes; 380 reptiles; 122 frogs; 180 freshwater fish; 750 molluscs and 54,000 species of insects. The flora consists of about 20,000 species, including nearly half of the world's 12,000 species of Proteaceae, and 700 species of acacia, more than half the world's total. Trees that are synonymous with Australia are the eucalypts or gum trees.

Beyond the safe suburbs, at the far extremities of the bush – beyond even the black stump – there lies the outback. Stark and primeval, the arid land stretches to the far horizon, the sun a pitiless companion overhead. In the Simpson Desert the weary traveller can see a sign, written by either a sage or a humorist, which says, 'Don't spit. You may need it'. It is an unforgiving land and if your car breaks down, you suddenly realise just how far you are from the conveniences of urban life.

The outback is raw, untamed. It is the inland frontier of Australia where life is as it was a hundred, or even a thousand, years ago. There lies the flat, parched land – not actively hostile but sentient nonetheless. This is where the Aboriginal legends come to life, emerging from aeons past as rocks shimmering on the horizon come to concrete life on your approach, though they had seemed insubstantial through the haze of mirage not minutes before.

The first venture into the centre of Australia from Adelaide was the abortive expedition of 1844, headed by Captain Charles Sturt, who is quoted as having said that he found, 'a landscape which never changes but for the worse'. The Burke and Wills expedition of 1860 left Melbourne on 20th August to cross the mysterious red interior. Their party took with them twenty-three horses, twenty-five camels and three drays. Their stores and equipment included thirty-seven firearms and sixty gallons of rum. Although they achieved their aim by reaching swampland around the Gulf of Carpentaria in February 1861, tragedy awaited them on the return journey, when Burke and Wills died of starvation.

Visitors to the outback are struck by the heat, the brilliant light, the red earth and the eucalyptus trees. D.H. Lawrence, the English novelist, was appalled by 'the vast, uninhabited land and by the grey charred bush ... so phantom-like, so ghostly, with its tall, pale trees and many dead trees, like corpses'. However, to native Australians the land appears more friendly and familiar.

Certainly there existed a great drive in Australia towards federation, and the dream was enshrined in the slogan, 'A Nation for a Continent and a Continent for a Nation'. An Act of Parliament in Britain was required first; one bright supporter of The Commonwealth of Australia Constitution Act had suggested, 'Gentlemen, if you vote for the bill, you will found a great and glorious nation under the bright Southern Cross and meat will be cheaper'. The Commonwealth of Australia became established fact on 1st January, 1901.

Australia is a new nation, not yet a century old. In that time it has suffered the shock of war on several occasions: World Wars I and II, Korea and Vietnam. The Anzac spirit, branded forever on the nation's consciousness one April day in 1915 at Gallipoli, is something that is understood throughout the British Commonwealth.

In a famous statement in December 1941, Prime Minister Curtin said, 'I make it quite clear that Australia looks to America, free from any pangs about our traditional links of friendship to Britain'. The Defence Force of today is, of course, the mainstay of national security, but the ANZUS Treaty ensures the support of the United States.

In 1872, the American conservationist Cornelius Hedges addressed himself to Congress, asking that legislation be passed to ensure that the Yellowstone area be maintained in its natural state for years to come. Today his words speak across the chasm of time and reach over national boundaries: 'It seems to me that God made this region for all the people and all the world to see and enjoy forever. It is impossible that any individual should think that he can own any of this country for his own in fee. This great wilderness does not belong to us. It belongs to the nation. Let us make a public park of it and set it aside ... never to be changed but to be kept sacred always'.

Australia has the honour of having opened, in 1869, the world's second national park, after Yellowstone – the Royal National Park at Port Hacking, to the south of Sydney. Today, nearly thirty million hectares, approximately four per cent of the country's total area, is reserve land or national park. These areas provide ideal places for relaxation and entertainment, much appreciated by the Australian with his native love of the great outdoors. They are also regions of solitude and respite from the cares and tribulations of twentieth-century life; oases for the troubled spirit when 'the world is too much with us'.

The parks are also the last redoubt for the beleaguered wildlife of the continent. They demonstrate the tremendous variety of climatic conditions, which many never get to know in a landscape famed for its deserts. From frozen snows to tropical rainforests and the Great Barrier Reef, the rich natural heritage of the nation relies on the efforts of conservationists to maintain the ecosystem in the face of relentless commercial expansion, motivated only by the economic necessities of the moment.

This great land has remained largely unspoilt since the dawn of time. It is a unique, amazing country and its future will be the fruition of the seeds sown by its people both now and in its history, which Mark Twain described as, 'full of surprises, and adventures, and incongruities, and contradictions, and incredibilities but they are all true ...' Well, truth is multifaceted, and Australia is a land of endless diversity where every person's dreams and ambitions can come true.

The brooding, wind-gouged face of Ayers Rock, in the outback.

The Olgas **right**, massive domed rocks, lie thirty-two kilometres west of Ayers Rock **overleaf** in the outback.

**Right**: Ellery Creek. **Above**: Standley Chasm, and **facing page top** Glen Helen Gorge, both situated in the Macdonnell Ranges, a little over eighty kilometres from Alice Springs. Standley Chasm is a sheer-walled feature, the sun only penetrating to its depths at midday. **Facing page bottom**: Ormiston National Park, where a tributary of the Finke River cuts through the Macdonnell Ranges below Mount Sonder.

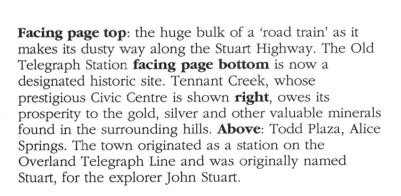

**Facing page top**: the huge bulk of a 'road train' as it makes its dusty way along the Stuart Highway. The Old Telegraph Station **facing page bottom** is now a designated historic site. Tennant Creek, whose prestigious Civic Centre is shown **right**, owes its prosperity to the gold, silver and other valuable minerals found in the surrounding hills. **Above**: Todd Plaza, Alice Springs. The town originated as a station on the Overland Telegraph Line and was originally named Stuart, for the explorer John Stuart.

Alice Springs, uniquely situated at the very heart of the continent, today serves as the ideal base from which to explore the Red Centre.

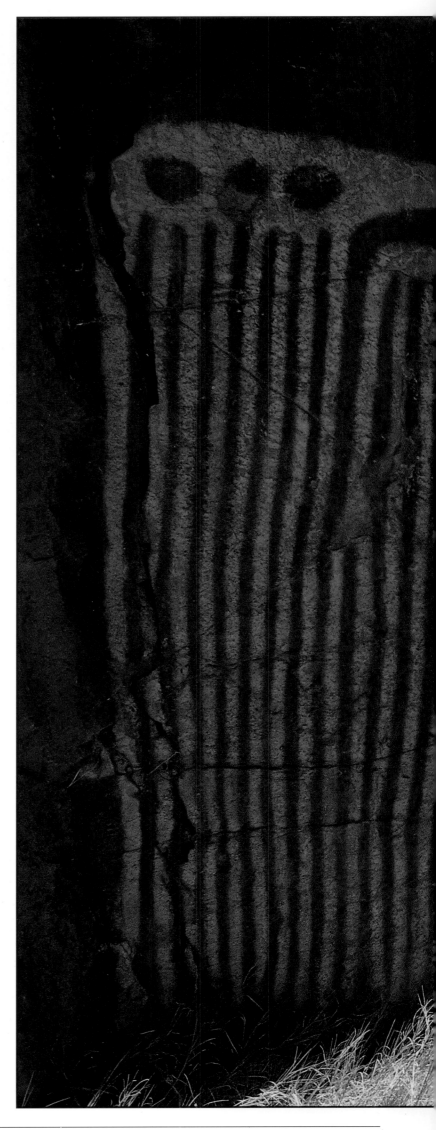

At Emily Gap **above**, near Alice Springs, remarkable Aboriginal rock paintings **right** decorate the sheer rock face.

Originally named Palmerston, Darwin **these pages** was eventually renamed in honour of the great naturalist and scientist Charles Darwin. Today, Darwin is one of Australia's most cosmopolitan cities, home to people from widely differing racial and cultural backgrounds. **Facing page top**: a cooling fountain outside the Law Courts. **Facing page bottom**: the Reserve Bank of Australia. **Top**: the modern casino overlooking the Timor Sea at Mindil Beach.

**Above**: the East Alligator River, which makes its way through Arnhem Land before flowing into Van Diemen Gulf. **Left**: Jim Jim Falls, and **facing page** Twin Falls, in Kakadu National.Park **overleaf**.

**Facing page**: a jetty **top** and pelicans **bottom** on the beach at Broome, on the Great Northern Highway. At the turn of the century, Broome was a boisterous pearling port. Kununurra **above** is at the heart of a vast irrigation project centred on the Ord River.

Hamersley Range National Park contains a series of high, rugged mountains, spectacular gorges, pools **facing page** and waterfalls. Kalbarri National Park lies north of Geraldton and is famed for its coloured rocks **right**, the appearance of which is due to the beds of red sandstone that underlie the region. The brilliant colours of the rocks **above** in the Hamersley Range attract thousands of tourists to visit the area every year.

A few miles north of Perth is Yanchep National Park, famed for its magnificent coastal scenery. Much further north is the sheep station **overleaf** that lies inland from Jurien, in a landscape considered the most beautiful in the state.

The modern city of Perth, with its ever-changing skyline **above and facing page**, is vastly different from the assortment of pioneer buildings known to Captain Stirling in 1829. **Left**: the War Memorial, King's Park, Perth.

Perth's bustling shopping centre **these pages** is an indication of the wealth that has come to the city as a result of its industry and increasing population. There is, as in most modern cities, a considerable mixture of the old and the new. **Facing page and right**: Hay Street Mall. **Above**: City Arcade.

Albany **above** has two claims to fame as the oldest town in the largest state. It may have a third, as it is considered one of the most picturesque towns in Western Australia, with spectacular views outwards over the coast and, inland, towards the Stirling and Porongurup ranges. **Right**: Bunbury, the state's third largest urban area, and a popular tourist resort.

**Facing page:** the truly remarkable, fifteen-metre-high formation known as Wave Rock **top**, three kilometres from Hyden, in Western Australia's wheat growing area. Equally fascinating is the beautiful Jewel Cave **bottom**, near Augusta. **Above**: the unspoilt natural beauty of the coast at Wyadup. **Right**: Diamond Tree Fire Lookout, nine kilometres south of Manjimup, affords wonderful views of the surrounding countryside. **Overleaf**: the Pinnacle Desert, Nambung National Park.

Historic buildings line the main streets of York **above**, and Kalgoorlie **right**. York is the oldest of Australia's inland towns and Kalgoorlie is reputedly the richest gold mining area in the world, centred as it is on the Golden Mile.

At Coober Pedy **above**, many of the homes, stores, and even churches have been cut from the solid rock to afford some relief from the unrelenting heat. **Facing page**: the Eyre Highway, stretching far into the distance across the outback.

Port Lincoln **above** is situated on Boston Bay. The area boasts magnificent scenery and is becoming increasingly popular with tourists. Another popular resort is Tumby Bay **right**, whose white sand and long, crescent-shaped beach is a famous attraction. **Overleaf**: the coast near Elliston.

**Facing page top**: the vast ore-mining area known as Iron Knob, situated deep in the interior of South Australia. **Facing page bottom**: a lone truck thunders along the endless miles of the Lincoln Highway. The most northerly port in the state, Port Augusta **above** lies at the head of Spencer Gulf. A thriving industrial centre, Port Augusta's position makes it an ideal stopping point for all east-west travellers and it is an important supply base for the vast expanse of the outback. Created to preserve the magnificent scenery, as well as the varied flora and fauna to be found there, the Flinders Ranges National Park **overleaf** covers a considerable area of the region north of Hawker.

The Barossa Valley **these pages and overleaf** lies about fifty kilometres from Adelaide. Enjoying a Mediterranean climate, it is Australia's most famous fruit growing and, particularly, wine producing area. There are echoes of its European influence not only in the vineyards themselves, but also in the imposing chateaux **above**.

South Australia is known as the Festival State and, biennially since 1960, Adelaide has become, for a month, the cultural centre of Australia as it presents its Festival of Arts. The success of the festival produced a need for a permanent site for the many events and performances staged, and this need led to the construction of the internationally acclaimed Festival Centre, which features an open-air amphitheatre, two drama theatres and a multi-purpose theatre.

A unique pedestrian thoroughfare, Rundle Mall **above and facing page** provides ideal conditions for Adelaide's shoppers, with trees, fruit and flower stalls and, of course, an excellent range of shops. The architecture is varied, the modern coexisting side by side with the traditional. **Left**: the Governor's Residence. Superbly situated beyond Pennington Gardens, stands St Peter's Cathedral **overleaf**, widely acknowledged as one of Australia's finest cathedrals.

**Right**: picturesque Hobart, Tasmania's capital, viewed from Lindisfarne, a suburb of the city. **Overleaf**: Hobart and its magnificent harbour on the broad Derwent estuary, seen from the slopes of Mount Nelson.

The centre of a thriving agricultural region, Launceston **facing page**, situated at the confluence of the Tamar and North and South Esk rivers, is Tasmania's second city. **Above**: the oldest bridge in Australia spans the Coal River at Richmond. Built in 1823 using convict labour, the bridge is only one of several historic structures in the town. **Right**: Gunpowder Mill, set in an old quarry just outside Launceston, and part of the famous Penny Royal Complex, a major tourist attraction.

**Above**: the beautiful rolling countryside and farmland of northern Tasmania, some of the most productive in the state. **Facing page**: hop fields **top** near Glenora, in the Derwent Valley, and a horse **bottom** grazing near Branxholm. **Overleaf**: sheep in an idyllic pastoral setting near Ouse.

**Facing page**: Geelong **top**, Victoria's largest provincial city, and Lorne **bottom**, one of its finest coastal resorts. **Above**: looking west from the Great Ocean Road, along Victoria's southwest coast. The road starts at Torquay and snakes along the coastline until it cuts inland at Peterborough.

These pages: the immense power of the ocean and the magnificence of Victoria's coastline seen to their best advantage in Port Campbell National Park, where the elements have created wonderful formations with evocative names such as The Twelve Apostles, Razorback Rock and Island Archway. **Overleaf**: Bridgewater Bay, near Portland.

Within the Grampians lies the McKenzie River and the
McKenzie Falls **above**. **Facing page top**: the famous
blowholes and petrified forest in the coastal reserve at
Cape Bridgewater. **Facing page bottom**: the road from
Port Fairy to Crags.

The Mildura Workingman's Club boasts one of the longest bars **facing page top** in the world. **Facing page bottom**: a vineyard near Mildura. Dusk falls over Echuca **above**, which is situated at the junction of the Goulburn, Campaspe and Murray rivers. **Right**: The Mall in Bendigo, where gold mining began in 1851 and continued for 100 years. **Overleaf**: near Echuca lie the riverboats *Canberra* and *Pride of the Murray*.

**Above**: *Puffing Billy* offers scenic rides in the Blue
Dandenongs. **Facing page**: Sovereign Hill, Ballarat,
recreates a time not too long ago, when the discovery of
gold turned this small rural settlement into a gold rush
town.

Facing page top: Melbourne's Yarra River, spanned by the elegant Princes Bridge which links Swanston Street and St Kilda Road. A variety of architectural styles is to found in Melbourne, with new buildings in both Bourke Street Mall **facing page bottom** and the modern Collins Place shopping and business centre **right** contrasting with those of an earlier time, such as Flinders Street Station **above**.

The ultra-modern lines of Melbourne's Victorian Arts
Centre **above** distinctly echo the traditional form and
style of the traditional St Patrick's Cathedral **facing page**.
Built in 1880, the Exhibition Building **overleaf** is set in
the delightful Carlton Gardens.

Facing page top: the Melbourne Cup, held at Flemington Racecourse on the first Tuesday in November. An expectant crowd begins to gather at the tennis courts **facing page bottom** in the suburb of Kooyong. **Above**: the popular beach at Sandringham, with its colourful crop of beach umbrellas and sun-bronzed bodies.

In addition to the superb scenery, which includes
Pyramid Rock **above**, and The Nobbies **facing page
top**, Phillip Island has another popular tourist attraction
in the large number of fairy penguins that make their
home there. **Facing page bottom**: the foreshore at
Seaspray, along Ninety Mile Beach. **Overleaf**: Norman
Bay, particularly valued for its safe bathing.

A hang-glider soars high above the shoreline at Stanwell Park.

Canberra **these pages**, Australia's capital, situated in the Molonglo Valley, is often referred to as 'the showplace of the nation'. **Facing page**: Parliament House **top**, opened in 1927, and the House of Representatives **bottom**. A rainbow plays in the spray of the fountain **above** in Lake Burley Griffin, with the Captain Cook memorial in the foreground. **Right**: the telecommunications tower on Black Mountain. **Overleaf**: the magnificent ski slopes of Perisher Valley in the Snowy Mountains.

**Above**: the magnificent sweep of sand and scenery at McKenzies Beach. **Facing page**: fishing in the sunset-gilded waters of Batemans Bay, with the silhouette of the Clyde River Bridge in the background.

**Facing page**: Wagga Wagga, one of the largest cities west of Canberra. **Above**: a peaceful scene at the confluence of the Murray and Darling rivers, near Wentworth. **Right**: bunches of grapes laid on racks to dry for raisins.

**Above**: the parched and inhospitable landscape of the New South Wales outback. **Facing page**: deserted in 1889, the ghost town of Silverton lies on the road to Umberumberka Reservoir. **Overleaf**: White Cliffs, in the northwestern part of New South Wales, where a few opal miners still work, living underground to avoid the intense heat.

The settlement of what has been, since 1966, the city of Dubbo **facing page top**, dates back to the 1820s. The renowned folk poet Banjo Paterson was born in 1864 in Orange **facing page bottom**. Near Bathurst is the Mount Panorama Motor Racing Circuit **above**, the venue for the James Hardie 1000.

As one of Australia's favourite holiday resorts, particularly for Sydneysiders, since the latter part of the nineteenth century, the Blue Mountains have much to offer. Their name comes from the drops of oil produced by the many eucalyptus trees, which lend a blue tinge to the area. Among the many famed sights are the Three Sisters **above** and Wentworth Falls **facing page**.

Offering shops on three levels, and housing two
revolving restaurants, the Sydney Tower Centrepoint
**facing page top** dominates the city's skyline. Sydney's
famed Opera House **facing page bottom** stands on
Bennelong Point, overlooking the harbour, and looking
for all the world as though it is about to set sail. **Above**:
the Opera House, with the equally famed Harbour
Bridge serving as a backdrop.

Standing almost underneath the huge span of the Harbour Bridge, Pier One **right** is now a leisure complex which includes amusements, shops and cafés for both children and adults. Calm waters and an equally calm sky, together with the graceful span of the silhouetted Harbour Bridge **overleaf**, create a peaceful scene in Sydney Harbour.

Although there are some thirty beaches within easy reach of Sydney, it is Bondi that invariably comes to mind, whenever Australia's beaches are mentioned.

On the varied coastline to the north of Sydney lies
Newcastle **above**, Australia's seventh-largest city, and
one of its major steel manufacturing centres. **Facing
page top**: Nelson Bay. Coffs Harbour **facing page
bottom** is known, due to its role in the trade, as the
capital of the Banana Coast.

In the area around Coffs Harbour there are many banana plantations **facing page top**. Inland from Port Macquarie, near Wauchope, is Timbertown **facing page bottom**, a recreated lumbering settlement where skills such as blacksmithing, woodturning and shingle splitting may still be seen. Inland from Port Macquarie are pasturelands **above**, supporting thriving dairy herds.

The spectacular sweep of the bay **left** that draws many tourists to Coffs Harbour. **Overleaf**: scenic Korora Bay.

The distant, purple mountains of Lamington National Park form a spectacular backdrop to the City of the Gold Coast **these pages**, the name given to the strip of land that lies between Southport and Coolangatta.

**Above**: the Brisbane skyline, with the gleaming towers of the city's commercial district. Now dwarfed by the modernity around it, City Hall **facing page**, of a much earlier date, is still Brisbane's best known building.

**Above**: a corner of the Moss Garden in Carnarvon National Park. Among Queensland's other varied splendours are Curtis Falls **left** and Cedar Creek **facing page**.

The peaceful, historic city of Charters Towers is one of the state's gold rush towns and, in its heyday, housed about 300,000 people. **Facing page top**: the city's Gill Street. Some seventy kilometres east of the city lie the remains of Ravenswood **facing page bottom**, where derelict wooden buildings and rusted machinery serve only to remind the visitor of the town's former bustle and activity. **Above**: the Heritage Tavern in Rockhampton and **overleaf** a dramatic view of Mount Isa, the country's major mining town and the most important industrial centre in northwest Queensland.

In spite of the impression that might be gained from this tranquil scene, Townsville is Queensland's third city and a major port, handling most of the mineral output from the Mount Isa mines.

**Above**: reaping the state's sugar cane harvest. **Left**: ripening fruit on a banana plantation, and **facing page** a field of pineapples at the Sunshine Pineapple Plantation.

Cairns **these pages** is Queensland's most northerly city and an important and prosperous commercial centre. The Cairns bulk sugar terminal handles much of the output of this important sugar producing region.

To the north of Cairns lie sun-baked beaches **these pages**, epitomising everyone's idea of Australia's 'great outdoors'.

The Great Barrier Reef **these pages** and **overleaf** is one of the world's great wonders. It stretches for 2,012 kilometres, from Gladstone to Cape York, and covers an area of 207,200 square kilometres. The marine life of the reef is unsurpassed but, as with so many of the world's treasures, both it and the reef itself are under threat from development and pollution.

Sailing boats and other assorted craft gather for a day's
sport and pleasure on Heron Island, Great Barrier Reef.